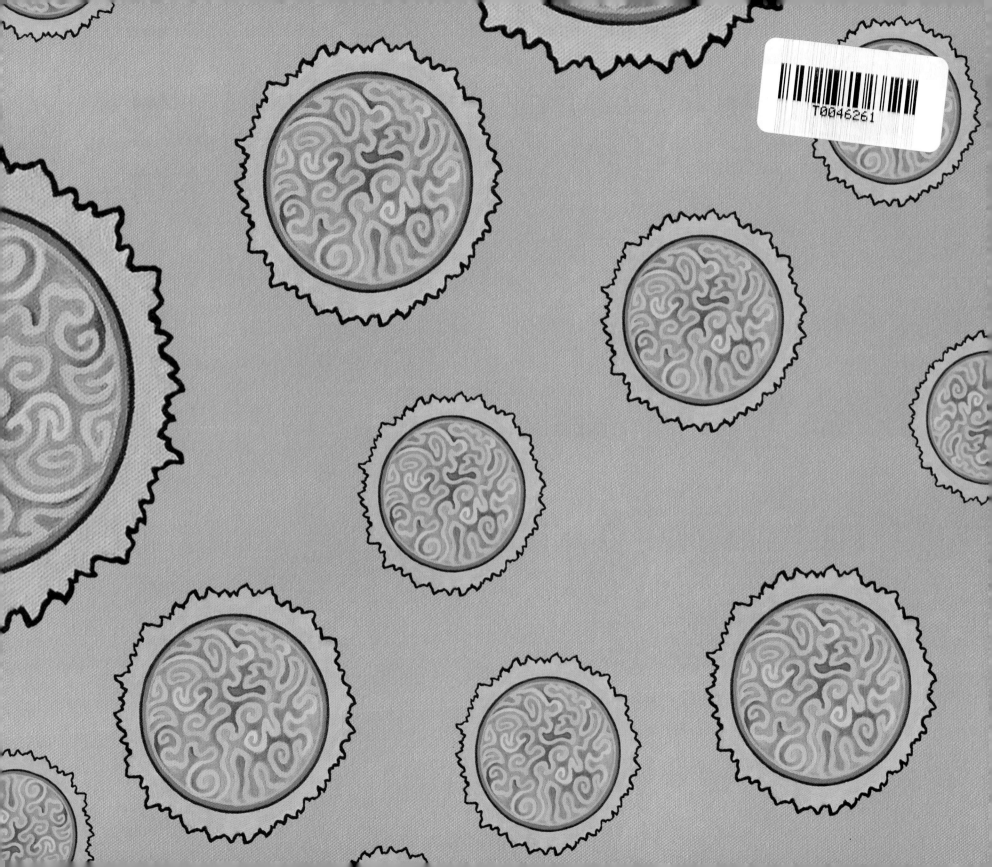

"We Learn from the Sun and every day, I learn from you, David James Manson. This is for you!"

Project Manager: Teddy Anderson
Design: Eden Sunflower (MWE Staff)
Editors: Allison Parker & Kaitlyn Stampflee (MWE Staff)
Text & illustration copyright © Medicine Wheel Education Inc. 2020
All rights reserved. Printed in PRC
ISBN- 9781989122396
For more book information go to www.medicinewheel.education

We Learn from the Sun

David Bouchard

Paintings by Kristy Cameron

We are taught how to live
When to take – when to give.

From our Elders we learn
How the Earth and Sun turn.

All their teachings are clear,
All their lessons are dear.

They are simple and fun
We just learn from the Sun.

First, we sit in a round,
Our legs crossed on the ground,

And we place our hands flat
On our Mother Earth's back.

With closed eyes, side by side
And our hearts opened wide.

We are many - yet one
Waiting there for the Sun.

We are small, and we're weak,
Like the Wolf, yet unique.

We are humble. It's fun
When we learn from the Sun.

The sun rises each day
In the East as we pray.

It is huge, it is strong,
We are not big, that is wrong.

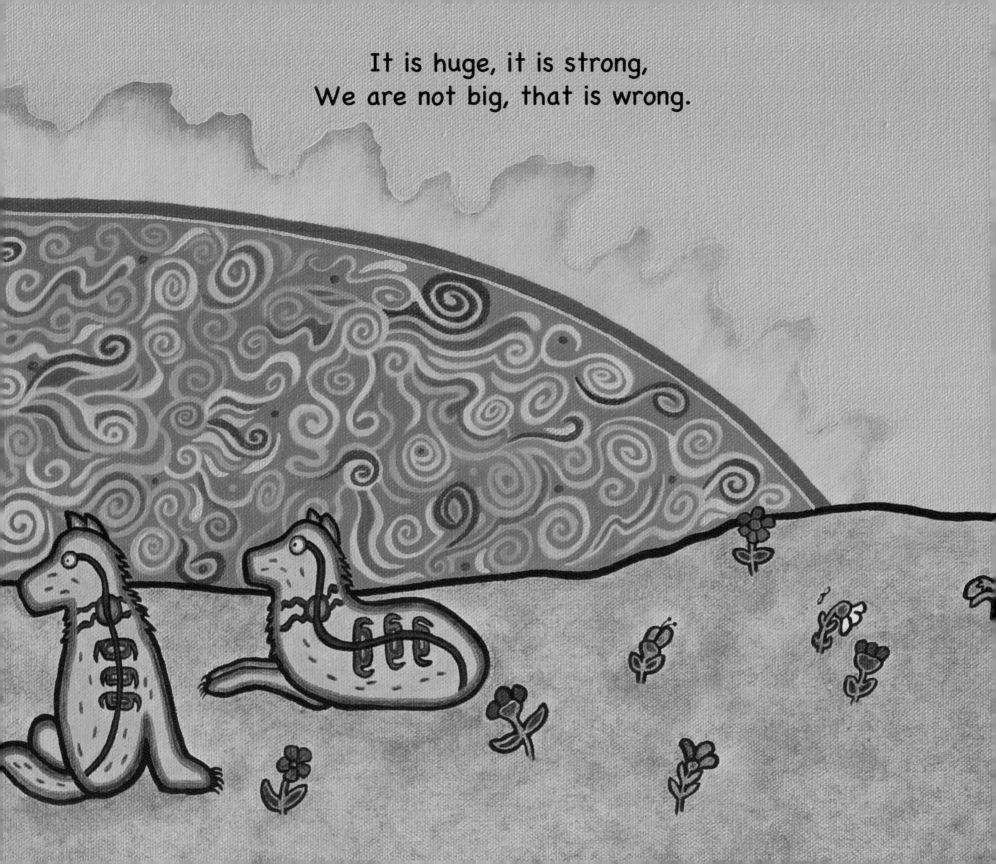

When the Sun's South we see
We have gifts, you and me.

We're unique, every one.
We learn that from the Sun.

When we look to the West,
Where the Sun goes to rest,

We are taught to respect
From the old to the nest.

Then we turn to the North,
And our courage comes forth.

Bear and landscape are white,
We find strength to do right.

Next, we turn our heads high
To our Father the Sky,

And hear Beaver advise
that we need to "Be Wise."

We are told to look down,
Mother Earth is the ground.

She's the tree - she is snow,
Where we're from - where we'll go.

When we look deep inside
In our hearts Eagle flies.

She is up there above,
Teaching us how to love.

You can learn how to live,
When to take – when to give.

You will find that it's fun
When you learn from the Sun.

Seven Sacred Teachings

Sacred Teaching (Ojibwe)
Animal, Colour, Direction

Humility (Dibaadendizowin)
Wolf, Yellow, East

Honesty (Gwayakowaadiziwin)
Raven, Red, South

Respect (Manaaji'iwewin)
Buffalo, Black, West

Courage (Zoongide'ewin)
Bear, White, North

Wisdom (Nibwaakaawin)
Beaver, Blue, Father Sky

Truth (Debwewin)
Turtle, Green, Mother Earth

Love (Zaagi'idiwin)
Eagle, Violet, Our Heart

Source: *Seven Sacred Teachings*

Books for ages 7-12 (available in English and French)

Educational lesson plans and posters available online!

Books for ages 4-6 (available in English)

Contact us:

Website: www.medicinewheel.education
Email: info@medicinewheel.education
Phone: 1-877-422-0212

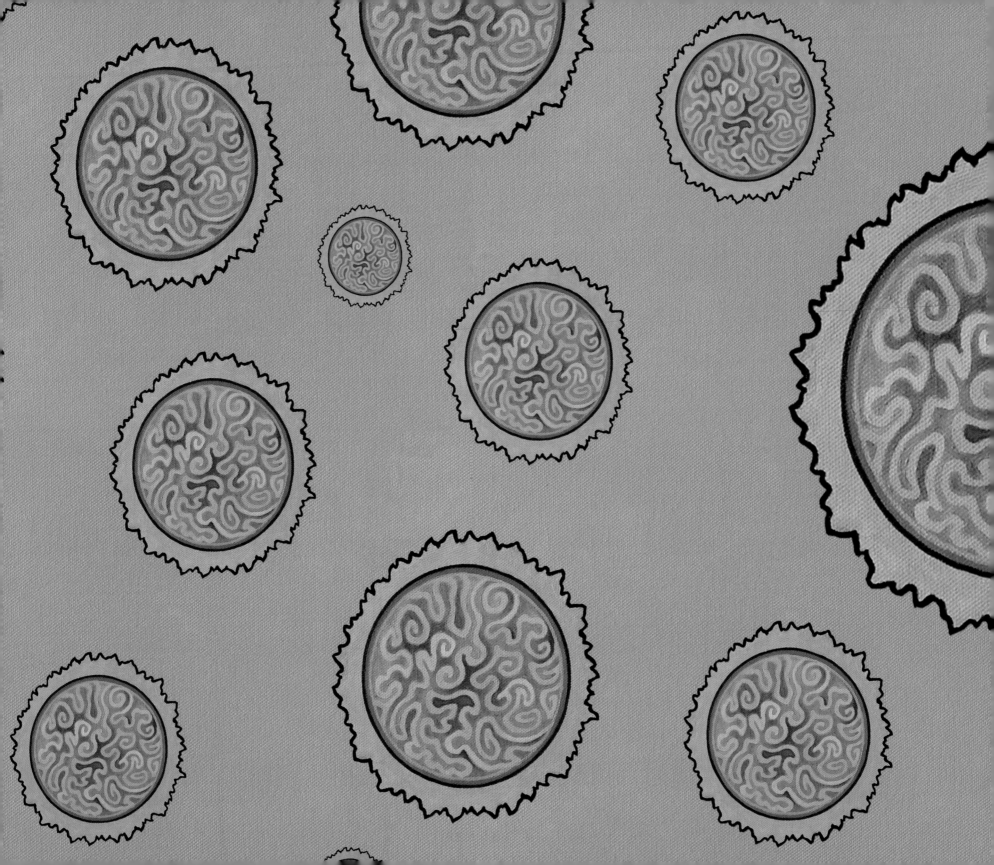